GEORGE
WASHINGTON

By CALISTA McCABE COURTENAY

ILLUSTRATED BY

A. M. TURNER

AND

HARRIET KAUCHER

George Washington

by Calista McCabe Courtenay

Published by Classic Books Publishing, Christoph Lymbersky, Luetkensallee 41, 22041 Hamburg. This title is in the public domain. Classic Books Publishing is a division of the Management Laboratory, Christoph Lymbersky, Luetkensallee 41, 22041 Hamburg, Germany

Publication date: April 2009, Hamburg, Germany

Registered with:

ISBN-Agentur für die Bundesrepublik Deutschland in der MVB Marketing- und Verlagsservice des Buchhandels GmbH

Bibliografische Information der Deutschen Nationalbibliothek
Die Deutsche Nationalbibliothek verzeichnet diese Publikation in der Deutschen Nationalbibliografie; detaillierte bibliografische Daten sind im Internet über http://dnb.d-nb.de abrufbar.

Interior & Exterior Design: © Classic Books Publishing

When ordering this title, use ISBN: 9781442130050

Table of Contents

George Washington

George Washington (February 22, 1732 – December 14, 1799) was the leader of the Continental Army in the American Revolutionary War (1775–1783) and served as the first President of the United States of America (1789–1797).

The Continental Congress appointed Washington commander-in-chief of the American revolutionary forces in 1775. The following year, he forced the British out of Boston, lost New York City, and crossed the Delaware River in New Jersey, defeating the surprised enemy units later that year. As a result of his strategy, Revolutionary forces captured the two main British combat armies at Saratoga and Yorktown. Negotiating with Congress, the colonial states, and French allies, he held together a tenuous army and a fragile nation amid the threats of disintegration and failure. Following the end of the war in 1783, Washington returned to private life and retired to his plantation at Mount Vernon, prompting an incredulous King George III to state, "If he does that, he will be the greatest man in the world."

He presided over the Philadelphia Convention that drafted the United States Constitution in 1787 because of general dissatisfaction with the Articles of Confederation. Washington became President of the United States in 1789 and established many of the customs and usages of the new government's executive department. He sought to create a nation capable of surviving in a world torn asunder by war between Britain and France. His unilateral Proclamation of Neutrality of 1793 provided a basis for avoiding any involvement in foreign conflicts. He supported plans to build a strong central government by funding the national debt, implementing an effective tax system, and creating a national bank. Washington avoided the temptation of war and began a decade of peace with Britain via the Jay Treaty in 1795; he used his prestige to get it ratified over intense opposition from the Jeffersonians. Although never officially joining the Federalist Party, he supported its programs and was its inspirational leader. Washington's farewell address was a primer on republican virtue and a stern warning against partisanship, sectionalism, and involvement in foreign wars.

Washington is seen as a symbol of the United States and republicanism in practice. His devotion to civic virtue made him an exemplary figure among early American politicians.

Washington was awarded the very first Congressional Gold Medal with the Thanks of Congress.

Washington died in 1799, and the funeral oration delivered by Henry Lee stated that of all Americans, he was "first in war, first in peace, and first in the hearts of his countrymen." Washington has been consistently ranked by scholars as one of the greatest U.S. Presidents.

CHAPTER I

WASHINGTON'S EARLY LIFE—APPOINTED AS SURVEYOR—FIRST TRIP INTO THE WILDERNESS—ENTRUSTED WITH MESSAGE TO THE FRENCH—1732-1754

The twenty-second day of February is a national holiday in America because, as everybody knows, it is the anniversary of George Washington's birthday. All loyal Americans love and honor him, the greatest man in the history of the Republic.

He was born in 1732, in Westmoreland County, Virginia, where the Potomac River flowed past his father's farm. The farm-house, called "Wakefield," was burned, but the United States Government built a monument to mark the place where it stood.

When "Wakefield" was destroyed, the family lived for a time in a home, later called Mount Vernon, in Fairfax County. But the real boyhood home of George Washington was a farm overlooking the Rappahannock River, where his parents went when he was about eight years old. His father, Augustine Washington, was a prosperous Virginia planter, and owned several fine estates.

His mother's name was Mary Ball. She was a beautiful and sensible woman, and a wise, firm and loving mother. She was his father's second wife and there were two little lads already in the home, Lawrence and Augustine, when she came to take the place of their mother who had died. Besides these two half-brothers, George had two sisters and three brothers. The two older sons were sent to England to school.

When George was eight years old, Lawrence returned home, having finished his studies. A great affection at once sprang up between them. George was a fine, manly little fellow whom any big brother could love, and he looked up to Lawrence as a model. Before long, Lawrence went away to the wars, serving under Admiral Vernon in the West Indies. His letters filled George with admiration and he at once became commander-in-chief of all the boys at school; they had parades and battles in imitation of those Lawrence wrote about.

George's father died when he was twelve years old, but, fortunately, he had a wise and careful mother. She taught him respect and obedience to authority; justice and courtesy to others; loyalty to God and his country. He had a high temper and a spirit of command, which she taught him to control. A few times only in his life, when greatly provoked, did his anger get beyond bounds. He loved and honored his mother deeply and never forgot her teachings.

George and his younger brothers were educated in the country schools of Virginia. George soon showed that he had a practical mind, caring little for poetry and literature. He liked mathematics and wanted to know about business and keeping accounts. He spent hours copying into a book the exact forms of legal papers of all kinds. He was very neat and accurate in his school work and learned the value of system and order. He never began a thing without finishing it. He never did anything without knowing the reason why. When he grew up, these fine principles and this skill and accuracy, fitted him to take a great part in the history of America.

All boys in those early days knew how to handle guns and manage horses. George was an expert rider and loved the life of the woods. Being exceptionally tall and strong, he was the champion athlete at school. It is said he could throw a stone farther than any man in Virginia. Besides, he was so fair-minded that the boys always let him settle their disputes and quarrels, knowing he would give every one a square deal. He was the admired and trusted leader of them all.

In addition to his mother's care, George soon had the loving advice and devoted friendship of his brother Lawrence. The war was over and that splendid young gentleman had come home, and had married the charming Anne Fairfax. His house, willed to him by his father, stood upon a hill overlooking the beautiful Potomac River. To this lovely home, surrounded by lawns and stately trees, Lawrence gave the name Mount Vernon, in honor of the Admiral under whom he had served. George spent as much time as possible here, where he met many persons of education and refinement.

While he was still a young boy, he wrote out for himself a long list of rules of politeness and good behavior. He had observed that older people do not like careless children, who forget the comforts and rights of others. As a result, he was well liked by his brother's friends. Among them were often military and naval officers, who told him stories of war and adventure in foreign lands. When he was fourteen, one of these officers would have appointed him midshipman in the British navy. He was eager to go, but his mother needed his help in the management of their property. So he continued two years more at school, studying mathematics, engineering and surveying.

The country was then new and wild and there was much work for land surveyors, whose business it was to measure off boundaries and describe the positions of rivers, mountains and forests in a piece of land. George learned to do this so well that by the time he was sixteen, he was appointed public surveyor of his county. His chief work for the next three years was on the vast tracts of land owned by Lord Fairfax, the uncle of Lawrence Washington's wife. Though very young, George was a great favorite with his lordship, who often took him fox hunting. George was a bold and skillful horseman and rode well after the hounds.

Surveying

The estate of Lord Fairfax, lying between the Potomac and Rappahannock rivers and extending to the Alleghany Mountains, had been given to his grandfather by King Charles II. These lands had never been settled nor surveyed. People known as squatters were now moving in and taking possession of the best places without permission. It became necessary to have the land surveyed, and these settlers either driven out or made to pay for certain definite parts. Lord Fairfax knew no one who could do this so well as George Washington, for he was strong and fair enough to deal wisely with the rough settlers. It was just what George wanted to do, and he gladly accepted the offer.

In March, George set out for his first trip into the wilderness. He was just sixteen years old, and it was his first big undertaking. George Fairfax, Anne's brother, went with him. They crossed the mountains into the lovely valley of the Shenandoah River. George's letters home were full of the beauty of the country and the richness of the land. After the first night, they found it more comfortable to sleep out under the sky than in the poor, untidy lodgings of the settlers. They lived on wild turkey and other game. They did their own cooking, roasting the meat on sticks over the fire and eating it on broad, clean chips.

They met a party of war-painted Indians, and for the first time George saw an Indian war dance. He studied the Indians carefully, for he wanted to understand their ways so that he might know how to deal with them. All through his life, he was kind and just in his treatment of these people.

The work of surveying grants of land took them long distances among the mountains and through the valleys. They traveled on horseback over the woodland trails, for there were as yet no roads. Sometimes they found the rivers so high that they crossed in canoes, their horses swimming.

George returned in a month, well pleased with his adventures, and Lord Fairfax, delighted with his success, paid him well.

The cordial, friendly, free life of Virginia pleased Lord Fairfax more than did the life in England. When he heard the account of the fertility and beauty of the Shenandoah Valley, he decided to make his home there. George laid out for him a fine farm of ten thousand acres. The long stone farm-house, surrounded by servants' quarters, stables and kennels, was located on a charming hillside. The place was called "Greenway Court," and visitors always found a warm welcome, whether Indians, woodsmen, or friends from the cities. Here George stayed when on his surveying trips and during the hunting seasons.

Until he was nineteen, George spent his time at his work, or at home with his mother or at Mount Vernon with Lawrence. The society of his home and friends kept him from being spoiled by the roughness of the wilderness. He was now six feet, two inches in height, with a fresh, out-door complexion, blue eyes and brown hair. He had attractive manners, he was careful about his dress, and presented a pleasing appearance. Through all his life, George Washington was a true gentleman.

He was so well paid for his work that he was able to buy several pieces of fine land. His noble character gave him a high place among the leading men of his colony. When he was nineteen, he was appointed one of four military officers in the colonies, with the rank and pay of a major, $750 a year—a considerable sum at that time.

Troubles had now arisen between the French and the English about the ownership of lands west of the Alleghany Mountains. The Indians, regarding the lands as theirs, took part in the disturbance. To protect her frontiers, Virginia was divided into four districts, each under a leader, whose duty it was to organize and drill militia. George at once began to study military tactics and the arts of war. This was interrupted by a trip to the West Indies with his beloved brother Lawrence, who was ill of consumption.

They had hardly arrived there when George had a severe attack of smallpox; though he soon got well, his face was scarred for life. He wrote home about the beauty of the island, the wonderful trees and fruits, and his social pleasures—dinners, parties and drives. For the first time in his life, he attended a theater. He visited the courts of justice and the fortifications; studied the laws, the soil and the crops, learning all that could be learned about the island. The trip resulted in no lasting good for Lawrence, however, for he died the following summer, beloved and honored by the colonists.

George was only twenty, but Lawrence left Mount Vernon in his charge, and the care of his wife and little daughter. The farm on the Rappahannock had been given to George by their father. These two fine estates, with the property he had bought for himself, made George a large land owner when still a very young man. The care of all this property and his military duties kept him busy.

During this time, the trouble with the French had grown more serious. The English, having settled the eastern sea-coast, claimed the lands to the west for their settlers. The French claimed the same lands by reason of having explored them first. The rich country lying west of the Alleghany Mountains, between the Great Lakes and the Ohio River, was the region in question. The French were planning to hold it by a line of forts from the Lakes to the Gulf of Mexico, and near the eastern end of Lake Erie, they had built two forts.

Governor Robert Dinwiddie of Virginia decided to send a message to the French commandant, Saint Pierre, warning him to keep off English soil. He needed someone brave and strong enough to travel in the winter, through hundreds and hundreds of miles of forests and across mountains and swift rivers; who knew how to take care of himself in the woods; who could get along with the Indians, and meet the French officers with courtesy and wisdom.

Of all the men in Virginia, the Governor chose George Washington, only twenty-one years old, for this dangerous and important journey!

So, late in the autumn of 1753, Major Washington set out for the Ohio River, accompanied by Christopher Gist, a brave and daring frontiersman, and an Indian chief called Half King, as guides, together with interpreters and a small company of trusted men. They traveled on horseback, and took with them tents and supplies for the journey.

As they proceeded, cold weather overtook them and the forests became almost impassable from snow. Traveling was so difficult that, when they reached the Monongahela River, they sent two men down the river in a canoe with their baggage. These men waited for them at the fork where the Allegheny River joins the Monongahela to form the Ohio. As soon as Washington saw this fork, he marked it as a splendid location for a fort, of which we shall learn more later.

Pushing on a little farther, Washington and his men reached a little settlement on the Ohio River, where Indian chiefs met him in council. He told them he had a letter for the French commandant and asked for their advice and help. Indians are very dignified and slow in their councils. They kept Washington waiting for several days. Then three of the greatest chiefs went with him to the French forts. These were in what is now northwestern Pennsylvania. It was a journey of many miles through snow and mud and took nearly a week.

Starting for the French Camp

It was almost the middle of December before Washington delivered his message to the French commandant, Saint Pierre. He was politely received by the French officers, with whom he discussed matters very tactfully. It took some days to prepare the reply to the Governor of Virginia. While they waited, the French tried, with presents and liquor, to coax Washington's Indian friends to leave him. At this time, the Indian tribes were in a difficult position. Both the French and the English were trying to get their lands and each seeking to win their alliance against the other. Washington reminded the chiefs that he had their word of honor and so kept them with him.

After receiving the French reply, the party started back home, going as far as possible in canoes. The rivers were swollen and full of ice, making the water-trip extremely dangerous. On Christmas Day, Washington began his long journey home—nearly a thousand miles through almost trackless forests. The horses became so tired that he and Christopher Gist decided to hurry on foot, in advance of the others, to the fork of the Ohio, leaving their horses to be brought later. They tramped several days, camping in the forests at night. An Indian met them and offered to show them a short cut. But he was treacherous and guided them out of their way and tried to shoot them. They escaped, traveling as fast as they could all night and all the next day.

At nightfall they came to the Allegheny River, expecting to find it frozen over, but it was full of floating ice and they had no way to cross. After working a whole day, with only a small hatchet, they made a raft. In trying to pole this across the swift current, Washington was thrown into the water and was nearly drowned, but he managed to get on the raft again and they reached an island, where they spent the night. It was so intensely cold that Gist's hands and feet were frozen. The next morning, they got ashore on the chunks of ice and by suppertime were in the warm house of a trader named Frazier. In a few days, they were rested enough to go on to Gist's home, where the Major bade his companion good-by and went on alone on horseback, through constant snows and bitter cold.

On the sixteenth of January (1754), Major Washington delivered the French reply to Governor Dinwiddie. He had been absent almost three months on his perilous journey, and you can imagine that his mother and friends were glad to see him safe at home again.

The Governor and the colonists were very proud of the way Washington had performed his errand. His wisdom in his dealings with the Indians and the French, his firmness, his courage and daring in the face of peril, had indeed been marked. He had not only done well what he had been sent to do, but he had thoroughly examined the French forts and made notes of the best places for English defenses. From that time, he was trusted with important duties.

As might have been expected, the reply from the French commandant stated that the land belonged to French settlers and that they intended to keep it. It was Washington's opinion that the French intended in the spring to take possession of the whole country. The Governor of Virginia tried to interest other colonies to help fight the French. When they refused, Virginia sent Captain Trent to raise a company of men in the western country and to build a fort at the fork of the Ohio River, where the city of Pittsburgh now stands.

Washington, now Colonel, was ordered to raise three hundred men and build a road to this fort for cannon and supplies. He succeeded in getting together one hundred and fifty men, who were poorly equipped, and without training. They built the road as far as Cumberland. Here, in April, 1754, they met Captain Trent's men in retreat. A French force of three hundred men had surprised them by suddenly paddling down the river in canoes, and planting their guns before the fort, with a summons to surrender in an hour. One young officer and fifty men could not hold out against so many. So they surrendered and marched back over the mountains.

Every day traders and settlers came by, hurrying eastward. They said the French had taken the place at the fork of the Ohio and were building a strong fort. They were coaxing the Indians, with fine presents, to fight the English. If the British were to succeed against the French, they required a good road over which to march an army. So Colonel Washington hurried the road building as much as possible, but at best he could make only slow progress in such mountainous country.

He received a message from the friendly chief Half King, telling him that a French force was on its way to attack him. With a little band of men, Washington made his way by night through the forest, in a heavy rain, to the camp of Half King. Indian scouts tracked the Frenchmen to a forest near a place called Great Meadows, where, in May, Washington and his men attacked them on one side and the Indians on the other. The Colonel was in the thickest of the fight and, for the first time, heard bullets whistling about his head. Ten Frenchmen were killed and twenty-one taken prisoners. Half King sent the scalps of the dead men, with tomahawks and strings of black wampum (small beads made of shells and sometimes used by the Indians as money), to all his allies and asked them to join the English.

This was Washington's first skirmish and it opened the French and Indian War that lasted seven years. Washington now encamped at Great Meadows where he dug rude trenches, which he called Fort Necessity. Supplies of food and ammunition were slow in reaching him. He had been reënforced with troops from the command of Colonel Fry, who had died on the way, and Washington was now made commander of the joint forces of about three hundred men.

The French finished their fort, which they called Duquesne (doo-cané). Then about nine hundred French and Indians attacked Washington. The English fought bravely, but Half King and his men deserted Washington. Being greatly outnumbered, he was obliged to surrender.

Colonel Washington led his beaten and discouraged men home, trying to cheer them while sharing their hardships. The campaign, fought against such odds, had not been successful, but Washington was publicly thanked for his bravery and hard work.

He resigned his commission and went to look after his mother's affairs. He soon settled at Mount Vernon and began work on his farm. His greatest desire was to devote himself to country life, but he was needed too much by the colony to be allowed to live as a private man.

Washington taking command of the Army

CHAPTER II

WASHINGTON APPOINTED A MEMBER OF GEN. BRADDOCK'S STAFF—FRENCH AND INDIAN WAR— WASHINGTON MADE COMMANDER OF VIRGINIA FORCES—CAUSES OF THE AMERICAN REVOLUTION— WASHINGTON A MEMBER OF THE FIRST CONTINENTAL CONGRESS—1755-1775

Early in the following year (1775), England sent out General Braddock and a thousand soldiers, trained in battle, to take Fort Duquesne and drive the French from the Ohio Valley. Washington was appointed a member of his staff.

The Indians fell upon their flanks

General Braddock was a brave and experienced soldier, but he knew nothing of warfare in a new country, amid great forests and savage foes. He knew but one way to fight, which he had learned in the orderly camps and wide fields of Europe, and felt that nobody could defeat his well-drilled soldiers. He thought Washington too young to give advice, and paid no attention to what he said. He looked with contempt upon the queerly dressed, untrained Virginia troops, whom he called "raw recruits." Instead of being friendly and generous with the Indians, Braddock treated them coldly and they left him.

With much difficulty, the army and its supplies were brought over the mountains and approached Fort Duquesne early in July. As they drew near it, Braddock's men put on their scarlet uniforms and forded the river, with bands playing and colors flying. It was the first time Washington ever saw a regular, well-disciplined army and he enjoyed the sight, although he wondered how their orderly ranks were going to fight among the rocks and trees. Fearing an attack from the woods, he wanted to send Indian scouts and Virginia rangers ahead. General Braddock admired Washington, but could not help laughing at his fears. So he sent his soldiers gayly forward.

Suddenly, they were attacked in front! With hideous yells, the Indians fell upon their flanks. All that General Braddock had learned of warfare was of little use to him now in the wilderness, but he was courageous and determined. Four horses were shot under him and he was fatally wounded. Before he died, he praised the Virginians, like a brave and true gentleman, and apologized to Washington for not heeding his advice. He left to him his horse and his servant. All the staff officers were killed but Washington. His splendid height and broad shoulders made him a fine target, as he rode about the field trying to rally the men. His horses were killed under him and his clothing was torn by bullets. An Indian chief said, "A Power mightier than we shielded him. He cannot die in battle!" The contest ended in a terrible defeat for the English. The regulars were useless and frightened. The despised Virginians were brave but too few in number to meet the enemy alone. The survivors retreated with the wounded to Fort Cumberland (Maryland).

Washington had been twice defeated, but his courage and wisdom were so great that Virginia had made him Commander-in-Chief of her forces. His tasks were heavy for so young a man—he was only twenty-three at that time! He did the best he could under many difficulties and raised and drilled a force of militia.

While facing a common danger, the colonies were not united then in any way, except under a Governor General sent out from England by the King. Washington had no authority over troops from any other colony, nor would officers commissioned by the King take orders from him. Naturally, all sorts of disputes arose and finally Washington decided to go to Boston to put all these questions before Governor General William Shirley.

Two other young Virginia officers rode with him. It was midwinter. They had hundreds of miles of mud roads to travel. They had fine horses and were attended by mounted black servants in livery. The story of Washington's bravery in Braddock's defeat was known throughout the country. When these three handsome young officers reached the cities along the way, they were splendidly entertained, for every one wanted to honor Washington. He wore fine clothes and his appearance and manners delighted all who met him. General Shirley received him with favor and granted his requests.

Word was brought that the French and Indians were attacking the settlers beyond the mountains. Washington hurried back to his command at Winchester. He was anxious to have the forces and supplies necessary to attack Fort Duquesne at once. But while the people were clamoring for protection, Washington was unable to help them on account of the unfair treatment of Governor Dinwiddie, and the indifference of England. His force was too small and untrained to make an attempt against the French; but he remained patient and cheerful and for almost two years, he stood by the people who depended upon him. Then William Pitt became prime minister of England (1757) and at once took an interest in the defense of the colonies.

Washington was ordered to proceed against Fort Duquesne. That French garrison had been weakened by taking men and supplies to the battle-front on the north, where they were being defeated by the British. Before Washington reached the fort, the commandant set fire to it and fled. Washington planted the British flag upon the still smoking ruins and on the same site built Fort Pitt, which he named in honor of the great English statesman. This is where the city of Pittsburgh now stands. Thus ended the French occupation of the Ohio Valley.

The many cares and hardships Washington had suffered had made him ill and he returned to Mount Vernon, hoping that his military life was over. He was greatly loved and honored by his soldiers and his fellow countrymen.

When Washington was twenty-seven years old, he married a charming young widow, Mrs. Martha Custis. The wedding took place January 6, 1759.

Mrs. Custis had a little girl, Martha, four years old, and a little boy, John, who was six. Washington dearly loved these children, whom he taught and trained with great care. He and his wife were great favorites socially and at their home (Mount Vernon) they entertained many guests. Here the Custis children met many of the prominent men of those days.

One of these visitors was Louis Philippe, the exiled King of France. Noticing how many letters Washington wrote, he asked him if he were not afraid of writing something he might regret. Washington answered that he was careful never to do or say a thing he could afterward be sorry for.

Washington kept fine horses and dogs and was very fond of hunting. Although busy with the care of his great farms and his wife's large estate, he found time to follow the hounds. His wisdom and honesty were so trusted that, aside from his own affairs, other people gave him charge of theirs. He was often called upon to settle disputes, thus preventing law-suits. He was a member of the Virginia Legislature, then called the House of Burgesses, of which he attended every meeting and was careful to know all about the affairs of the colony. When he first took his seat in the Legislature, he was thanked for his military service to the colony. He rose to reply, but could only blush and stammer. The speaker said, "Sit down, Mr. Washington, your modesty equals your valor!"

For fifteen years, Washington led a peaceful and happy life with his family. He was kept busy looking after his vast estates. But then again, the country began to claim his attention. George III was King of England. Under his rule, unjust laws were made for the colonies, which the wise men of America knew would destroy their rights. The colonies were not represented in the British Parliament (where the laws were made) and so claimed that Parliament had no right to tax them. Needing money, England laid heavy taxes on the colonies, which they would not pay. After much trouble, all the taxes were taken off except the one on tea. That was left to prove England's right to tax the colonies.

In the autumn of 1773, several ships were sent over loaded with tea, which was to be sold very cheaply. But the colonists refused to have tea at any price rather than submit to "taxation without representation." There can be no freedom in a land whose people may be taxed without their consent. From several ports, the ships were sent back. In Boston, a party of citizens dressed as Indians, boarded the ships at night, December 16, and threw all the tea into the harbor. This is called the Boston Tea Party. The same violence occurred at Annapolis, Maryland. To punish the city of Boston, Parliament passed a law that no ship should come in or go out of her harbor. The port was closed and business stopped.

The Boston Tea-Party

News of this was carried to the other colonies. In Virginia, a day of fasting and prayer was appointed. The people did not want to give up their liberties, for which many had come to America. It seemed, on the other hand, very dreadful to go to war with the mother country. The colonies were independent of one another, but knew they must stand together against the injustice of England. Meetings were held in each colony to talk matters over, and it was decided to hold a General Congress, made up of men selected by each colony.

In the Virginia Convention, Washington was one of the first to say that the colonies ought to be allowed to govern themselves, make their own laws and decide their own taxes. He was usually very quiet in all that he said and did, but the wrongs of Boston had so stirred him that he made a fiery speech. He said he would raise a thousand men, pay them himself and march at their head to the relief of Boston. He said he had hoped there would be no break with England and he shrank from the horror of war, but now he began to feel that it could not be avoided and if so, no sacrifice was too great to preserve the liberties of America for the millions who would some day call it their home.

He was one of several delegates chosen to represent Virginia in the General Congress, which was held at Carpenters' Hall in Philadelphia, September 5, 1774. There were fifty-two members, the ablest men of all the colonies. Someone asked Patrick Henry who was the greatest man among them and he said, "Colonel Washington, if you speak of solid information and sound judgment." These men met, not as members of separate colonies, but as Americans with one country and one cause. Each meeting was opened with a prayer. Not often, in the whole history of the world, have men had to decide more important and difficult questions.

For almost two months, they discussed all the points in which they believed they were wronged by England. They were careful and just in all that they said. They wanted to keep peace. None of them wished to be independent of England. Neither were they willing to submit to injustice and the loss of their rights and privileges. They wrote a petition to the King and letters to the people of England and of Canada. These papers were very fair and wise and showed the noble minds and loyal hearts of these early great Americans. They were not rebelling, they were simply declaring their rights. In reply, England only passed more unjust laws. The spirit of revolt spread through the colonies. Militia was organized; some were called "Minute Men" because they promised to leave everything and go to war at a minute's notice. Months passed in active preparations. Military stores were collected. The patriots were determined to face death rather than submit longer to British oppression.

Meanwhile, the British General Gage, stationed in Boston with four thousand British soldiers, decided to surprise and take, by night, the supplies of the militia in Concord, twenty miles away. Dr. Joseph Warren, one of the patriots, heard of it and secretly sent Paul Revere galloping out of Boston on a fast horse to awaken the people along the way and carry the alarm to Concord. When the British reached Lexington (about nine miles from Boston), they found seventy or eighty citizens armed and waiting for them in the darkness!

Early in the morning of the 19th of April, 1775, the first battle of the great American Revolution was fought (the Battle of Lexington). The trained soldiers of England soon scattered the handful of patriots at Lexington and Concord, but, as the day wore on, they were joined by other patriots, and by the night of April 20th, General Gage found himself besieged in Boston by a rustic army of 16,000 men. The news of the battle spread rapidly and spurred the colonies to instant and bitter war. Washington said that the once happy America must be drenched in blood, or inhabited by slaves, and that no true man could hesitate to choose death for himself rather than slavery for his country. He was at Mount Vernon when the sad news came, getting ready to attend the second Congress.

Israel Putnam

CHAPTER III

BEGINNING OF THE REVOLUTION—WASHINGTON MADE COMMANDER-IN-CHIEF OF THE CONTINENTAL ARMY—BRITISH FORCED TO LEAVE BOSTON—1775-1776

A Ragged Continental

At the second Continental Congress, held May 10, 1775, Washington was made chairman of committees for getting ammunition, supplies and money for the war. His military knowledge and experience enabled him to make rules and regulations for an army, and he advised what forts should be garrisoned. (Troops placed in a fort for defense.) It was necessary for Congress to take care of the army of 16,000 patriots that had hastily gathered in the neighborhood of Boston, and to appoint a Commander-in-Chief of all the forces of the colonies. They had to decide as to who in all the country, could best be trusted with this important and responsible position. All eyes turned to Washington. When his name was first mentioned for this place, he, with his usual modesty, slipped out of the room. But he was chosen Commander-in-Chief by the unanimous (all agreeing) vote of Congress. When told of his appointment, he accepted, though he said he did not think he was "equal to the command he was honored with." He refused to take any pay for his services, saying that no money, nor anything else but duty and patriotism could tempt him to leave his home. Having one of the loveliest homes in America, he gave up his comfort and happiness and risked all he had for his country. Congress also appointed four major-generals—one of them the brave old Israel Putnam—and eight brigadier-generals.

There were many men in Congress at that time whose names Americans can never forget. They did many wise things, but none was more fortunate than this choice of a Commander-in-Chief for the Continental Army. One of the members, John Adams, called him "the modest and virtuous, the generous and brave George Washington."

Washington's early life and training fitted him in a wonderful way for this great and difficult post. As a young surveyor, he had learned much about the country and how to make his way through forests and mountains. Later, as a commander, he had learned how to fight in the woods, and all the secrets of frontier warfare. With Braddock, he had learned that soldiers drilled on the parade grounds and battle-fields of Europe did not know what to do when hemmed in by rocks and brush and savage enemies in a new and uncleared country. He had also learned how to value and how to handle the independent, though rough-looking, soldiers of the backwoods. With all this knowledge and experience, with his clear mind and high courage, Washington was the most dangerous foe the British could have.

In June (1775), Washington, as Commander-in-Chief of the army, left Philadelphia for Boston. There was no time to visit Mount Vernon. He wrote to his wife, telling her to be brave and that he trusted God would soon bring him safely home. General Philip Schuyler and General

Charles Lee and a light horse troop went with him. As they galloped along the way, people came out of the farms and villages to see the great General. Washington, now forty-three years old, was very splendid and dignified in his bearing, yet always modest and quiet—a gentleman and a soldier.

About twenty miles from Philadelphia, they met a messenger from Boston riding a fleet horse and bearing dispatches to Congress. They stopped and heard from him the news of the Battle of Bunker Hill, which had just been fought (June 17, 1775). The British had been victorious, but not until more than half their number had been killed and the patriots had fired their last round of ammunition. When Washington was told how bravely the militia had stood their ground, he said, "The liberties of the country are safe!" He was not troubled by the triumph of the British, because he felt sure the Americans would win when properly armed and drilled. This news made him more anxious to reach the scene of action and he traveled on as fast as he could. He left General Schuyler to command the patriot forces in New York.

The Charge at Bunker Hill

On July second, he reached his headquarters in Cambridge, where he was received with cheers and the thunder of cannon. The men had so little powder that they could not give him a great salute, but they spared all they could.

The next day, July 3, 1775, Washington took command of the Continental Army under a large elm tree, which still stands on the Cambridge Common. The patriot army was a rather discouraging sight. The 16,000 men had been called together without any preparation. They were farmers, fishermen and shop-keepers. They had very little discipline or order and were in need of everything—arms, ammunition, food, clothing, tents, shoes. As yet they were not one army, but a collection of separate companies from the different New England colonies. Each had its own regulations, its own officers and its own interests. There were jealousy and often misunderstanding among them. After reviewing this army, General Washington visited the American forts strung in an irregular semi-circle around Boston, within which the British forces were besieged.

He found the men camped in rough board shacks, or shelters made of turf and brush, and dressed in the clothes they wore on their farms and in the villages. Here and there was a tent. No wonder the British, in their orderly tents and fine scarlet uniforms, thought they could soon scatter this mixed crowd! There was but one exception. General Nathanael Greene, of Rhode Island, had raised and drilled a body of men and brought them to Boston under fine discipline, with good tents and clothing. His camp showed what could be done. General Greene became one of Washington's most faithful and lifelong friends, and was one of the greatest generals of the Revolution.

In contrast with the undisciplined, ragged Continental troops were the trained British soldiers, commanded by experienced generals. They were well fortified in Boston and the harbor was defended by their warships. They felt no fear of the irregular line of posts with which the Americans thought to hem them in.

Washington at once began the task of organizing the army and teaching and training the men. In this he showed skill beyond almost any other man in history. He was beset with many difficulties, among them the jealousy and discontent of some of the officers. There was one general, however, who was always ready to serve in any place and put the cause above himself. This was Israel Putnam, the brave man who was plowing in his field when he heard of the Battle of Lexington. He left his plow in the furrow, unhitched his horses and galloped sixty-eight miles that day to Cambridge! He was nearly sixty years of age at the time. He was much loved by the army for his bravery and generosity and all were glad when "Old Put" was appointed Major-General.

Washington formed the army into six brigades of six regiments each. He wrote to Congress to appoint at once officers to help him. He wanted an adjutant-general to train and discipline the troops; a quartermaster to arrange for all supplies, and an officer to look after enlistments. The men had enlisted for only a short time and numbers returned home after this term of enlistment expired; so it was hard to keep the army up to fighting strength. The lack of powder was also a very serious matter and Washington sent to the southern colonies, asking for what they had in store.

He at once began to improve the defenses and strengthen the weak places. Soon a strong line of fortifications surrounded the city. The strictest discipline was required and Washington visited the forts every day. The arrival of fourteen hundred riflemen from Pennsylvania, Virginia and Maryland was a great help; among these were the stalwart sharp-shooters under Colonel Daniel Morgan, whom Washington had known in the French war. They were six feet tall and over, and dressed in hunting shirts and wide-brimmed hats. They had marched six hundred miles in three weeks.

The winter passed in drilling the army and trying to get powder. Washington was besieging Boston without any powder, though the British little thought that was the reason he did not attack them! All he could do was to cut them off from nearby supplies of food, but they sent out warships with men who plundered the coasts of New England. The people drove their cattle inland and fought the invaders boldly.

Mrs. Washington set out for Cambridge

Knowing that he could not return home, General Washington sent for his wife to come to Cambridge. Mrs. Washington set out on the long journey in her carriage, drawn by four horses, and accompanied by her son and his wife. (Her daughter had died in the meantime.) Colored servants in scarlet and white liveries rode beside the carriage. Escorts of horsemen brought them from city to city, until they arrived in camp, just before Christmas. It had been more than half a year since the General had seen his family and his work was made easier by having with him those he loved. The Craigie house in Cambridge (later the home of the poet Longfellow), was Washington's headquarters. Here Mrs. Washington helped him entertain officers and members of Congress.

The General was so busy that he was often obliged to leave his guests at the table, while his own meal remained unfinished.

The plundering attacks by the British upon the New England coast became so violent that, without waiting for Congress to act, Washington had several armed vessels fitted out. They were commanded by such brave sea captains as John Manly and John Paul Jones and were ordered by the General to defend the coast and capture British ships bringing supplies from England.

As the weeks passed, it grew more difficult to keep up the numbers of the army. The men grew tired of the long and uncomfortable encampment without any fighting. Had there been any powder, their General would gladly have given them fighting enough! All through the war, Washington was troubled and handicapped by these short enlistments, as he had to be constantly training new recruits.

In December, some Connecticut troops decided to go home without even remaining for their full time. Some took their guns and ammunition. This desertion was a bad thing for the discipline of the army, and sorely distressed Washington. On their way home, these men were made to feel what the people thought of their conduct, for no one would give them food, and their friends would not receive them kindly when they arrived. The day after they walked off, something happened that put new life into the camp. A long train of wagons came lumbering and jolting into Cambridge, with flags flying and an escort of soldiers and horsemen. What was in the wagons?—Cannon! and thousands of guns and shot and thirty-two tons of musket balls! Captain John Manly, of the ship *Essex*, had captured a large British brigantine and taken her cargo of munitions.

In spite of Washington's efforts to appeal to their patriotism, the soldiers still wanted to go home. They were sick of the discomforts of camp. By January (1776), only ten thousand men were left, and there was danger of the poorly defended lines being taken. But for some reason, the British made no attack. During this disheartening time, General Greene was a great help, with his courage and patriotism and cheerfulness.

In February, Colonel Henry Knox returned from the forts on Lake Champlain with a long train of forty-two ox-sleds, carrying artillery and ammunition. He had gone in midwinter after the supplies of cannon and lead captured from the British the year before and had performed his errand with daring and faithfulness. Then ten regiments of militia arrived and at last, Washington and his generals thought they had men and ammunition enough to attack the British.

General Putnam had fortified a hill north of the city of Boston. Troops were sent, on the night of March 4, to fortify Dorchester Heights, to the south from which Boston and the harbor could be swept by guns. That the British might not hear the noise of the wagons and pickaxes, the patriots bombarded the city all night. The ground was deeply frozen and the work hard. But Washington was with the men, everywhere helping and encouraging them.

When morning came, the British looked upon four forts raised as if by the magic of an Aladdin's lamp! General Sir William Howe determined to attack these new works. A storm of great fury arose and he waited. The storm continued all night and all day. The patriots used this time to strengthen their forts, and the British saw they could not hold the city against them; so they prepared to leave, taking everything with them that could be of use to the "rebels." They were allowed to embark upon their ships without being fired on, to prevent their burning the city. They sailed away to Halifax. After being besieged ten months, Boston fell into Washington's hands without a battle! Washington was thanked by Congress and given a gold medal in honor of the capture of Boston.

Washington Crossing the Delaware

CHAPTER IV

DECLARATION OF INDEPENDENCE SIGNED—BATTLE OF LONG ISLAND—BATTLE OF WHITE PLAINS—WASHINGTON CROSSES THE DELAWARE AND SURPRISES THE HESSIANS AT TRENTON—1776-1777

Let us now consider some events which had taken place elsewhere in the country. Before Washington had been made Commander-in-Chief, Ethan Allen, with the "Green Mountain Boys" (so-called because they came from Vermont, the "Green Mountain State"), had surprised and taken, without a fight, Fort Ticonderoga in eastern New York. Shortly after, Crown Point on Lake Champlain was captured by Colonel Benedict Arnold. The capture of these two British forts opened the way to Canada.

While Washington was building up the army and besieging Boston, an expedition against Montreal and Quebec was planned. General Richard Montgomery, who commanded a force on Lake Champlain, marched up to Montreal, which surrendered (November, 1775) without a struggle.

Benedict Arnold was sent, with about twelve hundred men from Boston, to join Montgomery's forces in the attack on Quebec. They were to make their way up the Kennebec River and through the dense Maine woods. Arnold was a brave soldier and led his men through hardships and perils, through snow and ice and over frozen mountains, until they reached Quebec. On the last day of December, with the ground frozen and covered with snow, the two American armies made a combined attack on the city; but Quebec did not surrender, though the patriots fought with desperate courage and daring. The gallant Montgomery led his men up the heights, dashing forward with the cry, "Push on, my brave boys! Quebec is ours!" A volley from a cannon killed him and scattered his men. The Americans suffered terrible losses. In the death of General Montgomery, America lost one of her bravest soldiers and truest gentlemen. He was deeply mourned in England as well as in America.

Benedict Arnold also was beaten back; his leg was shattered by a musket ball, but he bravely fortified his position and with five hundred men besieged Quebec. He wrote, "I am in the way of my duty and I know no fear."

As the weeks passed, the men grew weary and homesick. They suffered untold hardships from want of food, clothing and shelter, and from the bitter cold of the Canadian winter. Though Arnold and his men fought bravely, Quebec did not fall into the hands of the Americans. Their attacks were repulsed by the British forces in command of the city.

Shortly after the capture of Boston, Washington brought his army to New York, as he feared the British might take that city. He sent General Putnam to fortify New York and the Hudson River, and he followed, gathering troops on the way. When he arrived, he fortified Brooklyn Heights, Long Island, and put General Greene in command. He had only about eight thousand men to garrison the forts about New York.

The same troubles from short enlistments, lack of discipline and supplies had to be met. Washington was freely giving himself to the just and righteous cause of American freedom, and he would not be discouraged even by want of spirit and obedience in his troops. There was another difficulty. All over the country and especially in New York, many persons, called Tories, were still loyal to King George III, and Washington feared treachery from them.

The British fleet, however, had not gone to New York, but up to Halifax. General Howe and his army waited in Halifax for ships and men from England. With their help, he expected to drive the Americans out of New York and away from the Hudson River. England intended to crush the colonies and hired German troops, called Hessians, in addition to her own forces. It was now a year since the Battle of Lexington was fought and Washington feared that the war would be a long one.

He went to Philadelphia to consult with Congress. To succeed against the British, the colonies, he knew, must work together in earnest for their common liberty. The army must have regular pay and supplies, and the men must promise to serve as long as needed. Congress established a war office and ordered that the term of enlistment be for three years.

Washington returned to New York and soon afterwards a conspiracy (plot) among the Tories was discovered. Many arrests were made. A member of Washington's body-guard was found to be in the plot and he was hanged. While this was going on, the British fleet arrived in the harbor. There were one hundred and thirty ships. The troops—30,000—were landed on Staten Island. Washington was very uneasy with this large force before him and he knew not how many treacherous Tories about him.

For a year, the Americans had been fighting on account of unjust laws and taxes. But England had grown still more severe and unfair, until many began to believe that the only hope for peace and prosperity in the colonies was in their union with one another and their separation from England. Washington had hoped that the trouble with the mother country might be peaceably settled. But the time had now come when he urged Congress to declare the independence of the colonies and throw off the British yoke. While he, in New York, was facing foes within and without, Congress in Philadelphia was discussing this great question behind locked doors. Anxious throngs crowded the streets waiting for the decision.

At last, on the 4th of July, 1776, the Liberty Bell in the State House tower rang out the glad tidings that Congress had adopted the Declaration of Independence! Washington was overjoyed when a messenger brought him the word. On the evening of July 9, he had his army drawn up to hear the Declaration read before each brigade. He said he hoped that it would inspire each man to live and act with courage, "as became a Christian soldier defending the dearest rights and liberties of his country." The people of New York tore down a statue of King George and melted it into bullets for the army.

The British fleet arrived

There was not much time for rejoicing, however, considering that the British ships were in New York harbor. Among them was the flagship of Lord Richard Howe, Admiral of the British Navy and brother of General Howe. He came with a proposal of peace from England and tried to deliver it in the form of a message addressed to "George Washington." Washington, resenting this insult, refused to receive the message and did not accept it until it was returned properly addressed to "General George Washington." Congress thanked him for making the British respect the dignity of his office.

America had decided to be free at any cost, and while her cause did not look very promising, it was too late to talk about peace. Washington

45

knew his forces were not strong enough to defend New York. The enemy had its great fleet, and thousands of men already on land with thousands more coming.

Washington had brought the army up to fifteen thousand men, but hesitated to rely on this force. He was still troubled by jealousies among the officers and among the troops from the different colonies, although he tried to show them that honor and success depended on self-forgetfulness and working together for the cause. The militia could not be counted on and could be called out only for special occasions. Whole companies would leave at the end of their enlistment, even though they were greatly needed. We cannot always be proud of this fighting force, though it showed splendid courage when really in action. The men had not learned that a brave soldier does not quit, but patiently endures hardships. At best, Washington's army was too small to strongly fortify any one place about New York. He had no idea where the British would attack first, and so had spread the army out until it was a long, weak line.

On August 26 and 27 (1776), the enemy surrounded the fortifications at Brooklyn on Long Island. The Americans fought with great bravery, but were outnumbered and defeated. About two thousand were killed, wounded or captured. Regiments had hurried to their help from points nearby and most of the army was finally on Long Island. Fearing his whole force would be destroyed, Washington decided to withdraw to New York, which he did in the night, under cover of heavy rain, wind and fog. He had not slept for two days and nights and had hardly been out of the saddle, but he watched the men embark with all their belongings, and he himself went in the last boat. When the British soldiers awoke in the morning, they were amazed to find that the whole American army had disappeared!

Nathan Hale

It was important for Washington to know what the next move of the British would be. Captain Nathan Hale, a fine young officer, volunteered to act as spy. He succeeded in passing through the enemy's lines and making notes and drawings, but on his way back, he was captured by the British. On Sept. 22, 1776, this noble patriot was hanged. His last words, while standing on the scaffold, were, "I only regret that I have but one life to lose for my country."

The army in New York was in great danger of being surrounded and captured by the British, whose gunboats bombarded all the forts. More than half of the population of the city were Tories and several thousand of the militia had deserted. Washington was kind of heart and did not blame them too much, but he knew that his force was too small to hold the city of New York; so he began to withdraw to the northern end of Manhattan Island. The British moved upon the city and found it easy to land, because the soldiers, left to defend the first fort they attacked, ran off in confusion. Washington, hearing the shots, galloped into their midst and tried to rally them, but they scattered like frightened rabbits. Washington lost his temper, and throwing his hat on the ground, he exclaimed, "Are these the men with whom I am to defend America?" He would have been killed or captured by the oncoming British, if one of his officers had not seized the bridle of his horse and dragged him away.

The main body of the American army soon assembled in a strong camp on the rocky heights near King's Bridge, defended by Fort Washington. Here they were attacked by the British (September, 1776), when the regular Continental troops fought valiantly and proved victorious, wiping out the disgrace of the retreat which put General Howe in possession of New York. This success greatly strengthened the army.

The Americans had repulsed the British at King's Bridge, but Lord Howe sent gunboats up the Hudson River to cut off Washington from his supplies, which were stored in Connecticut. Washington thought he might be forced to surrender if he remained, so he decided to leave a garrison at Fort Washington and take the army into camp at White Plains (New York). A great many of his men were sick or wounded, and the hospital arrangements were poor and insufficient. The disabled men were lying in crowded sheds, stables and any other places of shelter that could be found. Washington did all he could to relieve their sufferings, and in a letter to Congress, he begged for better pay for the men and better supplies. He also urged that a call be made for men who would enlist for the entire term of war, however long it might be. A British officer wrote to a friend in London: "The rebel army is so wretched! I believe no nation ever saw such a set of tatterdemalions (ragged fellows). There are few coats among them but are out at the elbows and in a whole regiment, there is hardly a sound pair of breeches. How they must be pinched by the winter! We, who are warmly clothed, feel it severely."

The camp at White Plains was attacked by the British, with heavy loss on both sides, and Washington again withdrew his men in the night and entrenched himself at North Castle on the east side of the Hudson. The British did not follow him, and this left Washington in doubt as to what their next move would be. He left a part of the troops in camp, stationed a strong force in the Highlands to defend the Hudson River, and with the rest of his army, crossed into New Jersey, opposite Fort Washington. From this point, he saw General Howe capture Fort Washington and, without power to prevent it, beheld his brave men bayoneted by the cruel German soldiers. The supplies and the survivors of the garrison— about twenty-eight hundred men—fell into the hands of the enemy (November 16, 1776). Following this, Lord Charles Cornwallis led six thousand British across the river and attacked Washington's forces, obliging him to retreat across New Jersey, over the Delaware River and into Pennsylvania.

Washington had with him but three thousand soldiers, ragged and half starved, but they loved their Commander and were ready to make any sacrifice for him and their country. He had sent orders to General Charles Lee to bring reinforcements from the north, but Lee was in no hurry to obey. Lord Howe, who was anxious for peace, issued an order for all Americans to lay down their arms and go home; for Congress to break up, and he promised pardon for every one if the order was obeyed. A great many were faint-hearted enough to give up, even though America had sacrificed so much for freedom. But Washington was undaunted and remained true to his purpose to free the colonies. He cheered his suffering soldiers and, after securing reënforcements from the militia of New Jersey and Pennsylvania, he took his stand at a point across the Delaware River opposite Trenton. He seized all the boats on the river and when Lord Cornwallis marched into Trenton, there were no boats for his troops and they could not cross the river to attack the Americans. Leaving Hessian troops to guard Trenton, Cornwallis withdrew to wait until ice should bridge the river for him. These German—or Hessian—soldiers were hated by the Americans on account of their cruelty and because they were fighting for pay.

It was evident that the British intended to attack Philadelphia and General Putnam was sent to defend it. Congress took fright and moved to Baltimore. The British held New York and Washington knew the people would lose heart if Philadelphia should also be taken.

General Lee's forces at last arrived, though the General himself, because of his carelessness and laziness, had been captured on the way. With this reënforcement and with forces commanded by Generals Gates and Sullivan, which had joined him, Washington intended to surprise the garrison in Trenton. He divided his army into three detachments and planned to cross the Delaware on Christmas night, because he knew the German soldiers would be drinking and frolicking on that holiday. Washington himself led about twenty-four hundred men, with artillery, to a crossing at a point nine miles up the river. The night was dark and stormy. It was hailing and snowing and bitter cold. The river was filled with drifting cakes of ice, which imperiled the boats. The crossing was extremely dangerous and it took more than ten hours to get the troops and their guns on the other side. When he arrived, Washington found the other two detachments had not started, so his forces alone surprised the Hessians completely, captured Trenton and took a thousand prisoners!

Messengers were dispatched to call the army from the Hudson and to gather the New Jersey militia. When these forces were assembled, Washington again crossed the icy river into Pennsylvania, but returned and occupied Trenton a few days later. Lord Cornwallis, who had come down in a hurry from Princeton, planned to "bag the fox in the morning." But he found the "fox" had been too sly for him, for Washington, leaving his camp fires burning, had quietly led his army off at dead of night, by a rough and roundabout way, to Princeton. At sunrise (Jan. 3, 1777), he surprised and put to flight the regiment of British which had started out from Princeton to help Cornwallis at Trenton.

Meanwhile, Cornwallis awoke to find his "fox" gone and he set out for Princeton, arriving just as the patriots had completed the destruction of the bridge leading to the town. Washington pushed on, destroying the bridges as he went. His men were nearly exhausted when at last they reached camp at Morristown, where Washington established headquarters, so he could guard the road between New York and Philadelphia, and keep Cornwallis shut up in New Brunswick and Amboy (New Jersey).

Congress thanked Washington, and great soldiers all over the world praised him for the wonderful way in which he had led his soldiers out of the enemy's pitfalls and turned defeat to victory. Many colonists, who had seen no hope of success, now believed that Washington's generalship would triumph. Congress gave him full military authority and he issued a proclamation, ordering all who were loyal to the King to go to the British camp and all others to take the oath of allegiance to the United States.

At Valley Forge

CHAPTER V

RECAPTURE OF FORT TICONDEROGA BY GEN. BURGOYNE—BATTLE OF BRANDYWINE—BATTLE OF GERMANTOWN—BURGOYNE'S SURRENDER AT SARATOGA—WASHINGTON AT VALLEY FORGE— ALLIANCE WITH FRANCE—1777-1778

The fame of the American cause reached Europe and many foreign officers came over, asking to be allowed to give their help. Among them was Thaddeus Kosciusko, a military engineer from Warsaw (Poland). Washington asked him, "Why do you come?" "To fight for American Independence," he said. "What can you do?" asked General Washington. "Try me!" was the brief reply. Washington "tried him," and he proved a valuable help throughout the Revolution. Another who volunteered his services was Washington's devoted friend, the young French nobleman, the Marquis de Lafayette. Though scarcely twenty years of age, Lafayette loved human liberty more than home and friends and the easy life of the French court, and at his own expense, he fitted out a ship, loaded with military stores, and sought to aid the Americans in their struggle. Washington loved him for his fine spirit, charming manner and soldierly bearing. He became a member of the Commander's family and his name is honored by every American.

Marquis de La Fayette

The year 1777 was a very hard and trying one. Washington's forces were too weak to fight regular battles with the British. He used every device to make General Howe think he had a strong army, and at the same time, tried to convince Congress that he could not act for want of men and supplies. The British kept him guessing about what they would do next. Would they attack Philadelphia or the fort on Lake Champlain? He did not dare to withdraw troops from either place to strengthen the other.

General John Burgoyne, one of Howe's lieutenant-generals, arrived from England in the summer of 1777. He landed at Quebec and marched with eight thousand men, British, Germans and Indians, to Fort Ticonderoga. The garrison of thirty-five hundred men surrendered. Valuable stores were taken and the presence of this new army discouraged the Americans. But Washington only said, "We should never despair. If new difficulties arise, we must only put forth new exertions." He could not leave his own position, but he showed the greatest wisdom in arranging and locating the forces in the North. He sent his valued Virginia riflemen, under Colonel Daniel Morgan, to help fight Burgoyne's Indians.

For months, Washington had watched the British fleet in New York harbor and now it put to sea with eighteen thousand men on board. Would it go to Boston or to Philadelphia? Washington led his army toward Philadelphia, believing this would be the British point of attack, and soon after, the fleet appeared while Washington was camped at Germantown, near Philadelphia. The fleet sailed away, however, without making an attack and the summer passed in marching troops here and there—calling them out and sending them home again. Washington had a busy time watching Burgoyne on the Hudson and the lakes, watching Howe, who was occupying New York and New Jersey, and guarding the coast.

The fleet finally disappeared and, after a council of war, the American officers decided to leave Philadelphia and all march north together to attack the British forces in New York. This was such an important move that a letter was sent to Congress asking permission. The messenger who carried the letter was Alexander Hamilton, a mere youth, though he was captain of artillery. He was very small but so brave that they called him "the little lion" and Washington addressed him affectionately as "my boy." Congress approved of the plan to attack New York and the army was about to march, when it was reported that the British fleet was sailing up the Chesapeake Bay. Washington's army halted near Philadelphia. The Commander-in-Chief knew that there were people in Philadelphia who did not favor the cause of American freedom, thinking it foolish for the poorly equipped Continental troops to fight the British. To encourage the people of Philadelphia, Washington decided to parade the army through the city. He rode at the head with his staff. The men were poorly clad and had no uniforms, but their guns were bright and they carried them well. They made a brave showing and after the parade, marched into camp on the Brandywine Creek.

Washington and Alexander Hamilton

The British landed at Elkton, Maryland—about fifty miles from Philadelphia. Washington sent troops of light horse to ride about the country and annoy them in every way possible. One young commander, Henry Lee, of Virginia, was so daring that they called him "Light Horse Harry." He was another of the brave young officers whom Washington loved to have about him and who helped him overcome the difficulties that beset him at every turn. Washington spent most of his time in the saddle, watching the march of the British. His troops were unequal to the enemy in every way, and though the war had lasted more than two years, he had never dared to risk a real battle. The time had come when he must make a stand in the open or acknowledge to the world the weakness of his army. He had about eleven thousand men, while the British numbered about eighteen thousand. He appealed to his soldiers to do their best and make a firm stand in defense of their national capital (Philadelphia). The battle of the Brandywine was fought on September 11, 1777, and the Americans were badly defeated. Following this, Congress moved to Lancaster (Pa.) and the British, under Cornwallis, took possession of Philadelphia, which they entered dressed in their bright scarlet uniforms, the bands playing "God Save the King." What a contrast to the ragged Continentals who had marched there a few weeks before!

Washington did not despair. His courage and determination grew stronger in the face of defeat and he firmly believed his fortunes would take a turn. After resting his troops, he made a surprise attack on General Howe at Germantown. He was in a fair way to success, when a heavy fog came on. The Americans could not tell their own soldiers apart from the enemy and a panic took place. But Washington, who was in the hottest of the fight, was not discouraged even at this disaster. He had proved to the world that his troops were not afraid of the British army, and his men, in spite of their losses, were encouraged by this encounter with trained European soldiers. The English had looked down on the American patriots, but they were now beginning to find them worthy foes.

During this time, the army in the North had been busy. General Burgoyne had sent a force to Bennington, Vermont, to seize cattle and supplies, but General John Stark, at the head of the New England militia, completely routed them. He captured a quantity of guns and ammunition and hundreds of prisoners. At the same time, west of the Hudson, another body of British was defeated and their tents and stores taken by the Americans.

This was joyful news to Washington, and these victories served to keep up the spirits of the patriots and also to disgust the Indians with their British commanders. The militia, too, gained confidence, overcoming their fears and finding they were a match for the British and the Germans. Recruits flocked to the American camp in the North and Burgoyne was soon surrounded. In the great battle near Saratoga (N. Y.), he was completely defeated and surrendered to General Horatio Gates on October 17, 1777.

This splendid victory gave the Americans large quantities of military stores, but most of all, it gave them confidence, for they had at last beaten the British forces. The experience of actual warfare and the example of the trained soldiers had taught them how to fight. One of Burgoyne's officers said that when the Continental troops were drawn up to receive the surrender, they stood like soldiers, though dressed as if they had come from the farm or the shop. He was surprised to see how straight and strong and fine they were! General Gates ordered his men not to cheer or show any desire to humiliate their beaten foes, and this courtesy tendered him by General Gates was reported to Parliament by General Burgoyne when he returned to England. He was especially touched by it because he had needlessly burned some of the beautiful homes of the very officers who were so gracious to him. This courtesy was very fine in Gates, but he failed in his duty to his Commander-in-Chief, and in many ways was unreliable. He did not report the victory to Washington, as was his duty, and paid no attention to his commands. He did not send the troops to Philadelphia, as he was ordered, and he did not even return the company of Virginia riflemen until it was too late.

General Gates and his friends were doing all in their power to destroy the good name and the authority of Washington. They kept back troops Washington needed and then criticized him for not fighting a decisive battle. But Washington endured their fault-finding in silence, for he knew that an open battle with such a powerful foe meant certain defeat, and patriotism so filled his heart that it left no room for selfish ambition. He was not seeking personal glory, but independence for America. If General Howe had attacked him, he would have fought bravely, but he and his fellow officers knew it was unwise to attack the British. In many skirmishes, however, his troops showed courage and steadfastness, and proved they were making progress in the arts of warfare.

A few months before this, Congress had made some changes in the quartermaster (the officer who attends to supplies) and in the commissary (food) departments, although Washington had opposed the changes. The result was a bad mix-up in getting supplies to the army, and food and clothing spoiled and went to waste for want of wagons to carry them to the camp.

Winter set in, and the troops were poorly clad and worn out from hardships. There were not enough blankets to go around, and many of the men were obliged to sit by the camp fires all night and thus got very little rest. Washington decided to go into winter quarters in the village of Valley Forge, about twenty miles from Philadelphia. From here, he could watch General Howe's movements and be ready, if necessary, to defend Congress, which now met at York. On the march to Valley Forge, many of the soldiers were barefooted and they left a trail of blood on the frozen ground. To add to their suffering, someone blundered, and they were several days without food. Washington was blamed for going into winter quarters and not driving the enemy out of Philadelphia. He wrote to Congress, giving a full account of how he had been annoyed and hindered by those who should have helped him. He told them that nearly three thousand of his men were unfit for duty because they were almost naked, and two thousand more were sick for want of food and shelter.

During this cruel winter of 1777-1778, many men froze and starved to death in camp and hundreds of horses were lost. Washington, who was always careful about other people's property, was sometimes obliged to let his men seize food from the farmers. Congress did not stand by him. Some of the members were jealous of his power and his influence. General Gates was the popular hero after the victory of Saratoga, and a plot hatched by officers and members of Congress almost succeeded in putting him in Washington's place. Though Washington's plan had made the defeat of General Burgoyne possible, Gates claimed all the credit. Washington bore all this fault-finding and unfairness with patient courage. He kept his temper and devoted himself to his suffering men, whose endurance touched his heart. Fortunately for America, the conspiracy against Washington failed and the only result was to make his name and fame brighter and more widespread.

**Benjamin Franklin was
at the French Court.**

While the Americans in camp at Valley Forge were so miserable, the British, twenty miles away, were spending a gay winter in the homes of the people of Philadelphia. Why they did not attack and destroy the wretched patriot army was a mystery. After awhile, provisions and other necessities were secured and the camp became more cheerful. Mrs. Washington and the wives of some of the other officers came to join their husbands.

Baron Frederick von Steuben, a German officer, who had served in several wars and received great honors, was sent to America by friends in Paris. He offered to fight for the colonists without rank or pay.

Congress sent him to Washington, who realized that his experience would be valuable, and who asked him to drill and discipline the troops. Steuben was a wonderful soldier and after a few weeks under his direction, the army learned something of real military tactics, and how to work together like a great machine. He not only drilled them, but looked after their comforts and won their love by his kindness.

Not all the work for freedom was done on the battle-fields and in the camps. While Washington and his soldiers were skirmishing with the British and while they were encamped at Valley Forge, Benjamin Franklin, one of the foremost thinkers and statesmen of the time, was in Europe making friends for the American cause and asking help for the struggling colonists. The King of France made a treaty of alliance with him, which Congress signed May 4th, 1778. Three days later, it was celebrated in camp with thanksgiving and parades, and the news that France was to help the American cause thrilled every patriot's heart with joy.

CHAPTER VI

BATTLE OF MONMOUTH—PATRIOTS RECEIVE AID FROM FRANCE—RECAPTURE OF FORT AT STONY POINT BY GEN. ANTHONY WAYNE—WASHINGTON AT MORRISTOWN—SURRENDER OF CHARLESTON, S. C., TO THE BRITISH—TREASON OF BENEDICT ARNOLD—1778-1780

Molly Pitcher

General Howe had spent a pleasant winter and spring holding Philadelphia, but he had done nothing in the way of military service. He was now ordered home and Sir Henry Clinton took his place and was told to leave the city. While Washington was in doubt as to what move Clinton would make, messengers came from England with offers of peace for the colonies. They offered a large bribe to General Joseph Reed, a member of Congress. His scornful answer was, "I am not worth purchasing, but such as I am, the King of Great Britain is not rich enough to do it!" This was the spirit that won freedom for America.

In June (1778), General Clinton withdrew his army from Philadelphia and Washington marched his troops out of Valley Forge and followed him. Near Monmouth, New Jersey, Washington decided to make an attack. He sent General Charles Lee (who, by this time, had been released by the British) with six thousand men to start the battle, while he brought up the main division. General Lee, who never would take orders from Washington, commanded his men to retreat. Immediately Washington heard of this disobedience, he galloped forward, sternly ordered Lee to the rear, and with hot words rallied the men, stopped the retreat and saved the day. His presence and the courage he displayed ended the disorder and put new life into the men. An officer, who saw him at the time, said his anger was splendid and he "swore like an angel from heaven."

Washington spent the night upon the field, his head pillowed on the roots of a tree. At daybreak he arose to renew the attack, but the enemy had learned one of his own tricks and, as Washington himself put it, "had stolen off in the night as silent as the grave." It was at this battle of Monmouth that Molly Pitcher became a heroine. She had been carrying water to the men in action. At one gun, six men had been killed, the last one her husband. As he fell, she seized the ramrod from his hand and took his place. Washington was proud of her courage and gave her the rank and pay of her husband.

The love and respect in which the army held Washington were increased by his magnificent daring and splendid generalship in this battle. Congress thanked him "for his great good conduct." General Charles Lee, who had always been disrespectful to Washington and who had tried his best to harm him, was court-martialed for insubordination (disobedience) and deprived of his command. (Charles Lee was not connected with the Lees of Virginia.) General Lee was really a brilliant soldier, but he was ruined by his own jealous disposition. Washington treated him and all other enemies with the kindness of a great mind and a true heart.

After the Battle of Monmouth, Clinton took up his quarters in New York and Washington remained in New Jersey. Soon he received word that the French King had sent a fleet of eighteen ships and four thousand soldiers to help the colonists. The Americans were very glad of this, thinking that the British fleet would now be destroyed; but the attack of the French (August, 1778) was unsuccessful and they sailed away without having done much good.

We have spoken several times of the Tories who sided with the British. When the war broke out, the patriot settlers in the Wyoming Valley, Pennsylvania, decided they would join in the defense of the country and they drove all the Tories out of the Valley. Just after the Battle of Monmouth (June 28, 1778), while all the fighting men were away, these Tories got together seven hundred Indians and attacked the women and children. Before Washington could send aid, the whole Valley was laid waste. All the homes were burned. Hundreds were killed by the Indians and many more died trying to reach places of safety. This was followed by night attacks in different places, when sentinels were surprised and murdered by Indians and Tories. Indeed, all through the war, the most cruel enemies the patriots had were their Tory neighbors.

To guard against such attacks, and to be ready to meet the British at any point, Washington distributed his troops in a long line of camps and got ready to defend the country from Boston to Philadelphia. The Hudson River was guarded by a fortress at West Point. In order to call the militia out, he arranged a system of signals. On a high hill overlooking the British camp, sentries kept constant watch. If the enemy moved, warning was to be given by firing a big gun. When the gun boomed, fires were to be lighted on the hills within hearing. As soon as these were seen from more distant hills, other fires were to be lighted, until every hilltop blazed and all the countryside was roused and men warned to hurry to their rallying places.

Though General Clinton had a great army, he did not offer battle. He carried on an annoying form of warfare by sending out small bodies of men to distant places, to attack and destroy. In this way he plundered and burned villages on the shores of the Chesapeake and in New England and captured valuable stores.

"Mad Anthony" Wayne

While these things were happening, Washington planned to recapture the fort at Stony Point on the Hudson, which had been taken by Sir Henry Clinton, May 31, 1779. His plan was entrusted to General Wayne, called "Mad Anthony" Wayne because of his dashing bravery. Wayne took a small body of light-armed, fearless men, marched through the mountains and at midnight on July 16, stormed the fort and captured it. This feat was so well done that it is considered one of the great events of the war. Congress thanked Washington for the victory and gave Wayne a medal for his courage and success.

The swift and daring young scout, "Light Horse Harry" Lee, was with this expedition. After it was over, he asked permission to lead an attack on the garrison of Paulus Hook (now Jersey City), right under the guns of New York. Washington, who always admired courageous deeds, allowed him to make the attempt. Lee surprised the fort at night, captured a number of prisoners and made a successful retreat while the guns from the battleships were sounding the alarm. These two daring attacks increased the confidence and spirit of the Americans and gave the British more respect for them. Still, it was tiresome for the troops to remain month after month in camp, wondering what the enemy would do next.

Washington had more serious troubles. Congress was slow and often unwise in its acts. The people grew tired of the war, because business was suffering and the farms were neglected, and nothing seemed to be gained by it. Officers resigned from the army and men deserted. Washington was laughed at by the Tories and criticized by his friends. But he was patient and said, "We must not despair! The game is yet in our hands; to play it well is all we have to do."

Washington's greatness is shown not only by his skill in action, but by the patience with which he could wait. He simply would not be discouraged. Under such trials, he became "the best among the great."

The winter came and Washington took part of his army into a camp of log huts at Morristown, New Jersey. The sad story of Valley Forge was repeated here and the winter (1779-1780) was the coldest ever known in the colonies.

When the war broke out, there was, of course, no American money. Congress had put out some paper money called "Continental Currency," but it was worth so little that it took a great deal of it to buy anything. Washington was obliged to ask the states to give the army grain and cattle. New Jersey, where a part of the army was stationed, was very generous and the women knitted socks and made clothes for the soldiers.

The British went on surprising and killing small garrisons and plundering the country. In December, 1779, General Clinton sailed, with General Cornwallis and a strong army, to attack Charleston, South Carolina. They landed at Savannah, Georgia, and marched overland. Washington dared not go to the help of the Southern troops and leave the Hudson unguarded against the British army from Canada, which might descend upon it. General Benjamin Lincoln and Commander Whipple were, therefore, left alone to defend Charleston, which they did bravely, though it was bombarded on all sides by the British. They held out until their guns were destroyed and their provisions gone. The people were frightened into submission and on May 12, 1780, the city of Charleston surrendered, and Lincoln and his army became prisoners of war. Considering South Carolina conquered, General Clinton went back to New York, leaving Lord Cornwallis in command, with orders to subdue North Carolina and Virginia.

After their success in the South, the British made an attempt to capture Washington's headquarters at Morristown. The patriots of New Jersey rallied to the help of the army and drove off the British, who withdrew, burning houses and killing people as they went. Soon after this, the Americans were encouraged by the arrival (July 10, 1780) of a large French force under Count de Rochambeau (ro-sham-bo), who came to help them.

Early in the year (January, 1780), Washington had had the unpleasant duty laid upon him by Congress of rebuking General Benedict Arnold, who, though he was very brave and fought gallantly, had been guilty of several unwise acts. Washington greatly admired General Arnold and made his reproof so gentle that it was almost a compliment. But being called to account at all was more than Arnold could bear. He felt hurt, too, that Congress had promoted others and had only blame for him. This so enraged him that he proved false to the trust Washington had placed in him and false to his country.

After his rebuke, feeling that he had been treated unfairly, Arnold began writing letters to Major John André, a popular young British officer, in which he offered to betray the fortress of the Hudson. At Arnold's own request, Washington gave him command of West Point and an important part in a plan to attack the British with the help of the French. Washington had gone to consult with the French commander in Newport (R. I.), when Major André and General Arnold met. At dead of night, September 21, 1780, they went to a house in the forest to make arrangements for the betrayal of West Point. With letters and plans of the fort hidden in his boots, Major André rode back alone to New York. He was caught and searched by three young farmers, who were guarding their cattle against the outlaws who overran the neighborhood. They found the letters and knew he was a spy. André begged them to release him and made them all kinds of offers if they would, but they marched him off ten miles to the nearest fort.

A Messenger came to Benedict Arnold

General Washington came back from Newport two days earlier than he was expected. Lafayette, Count Rochambeau and Hamilton rode with him and they planned to go at once to West Point. Arnold was living with his family in a house several miles from the fort and Washington sent word they would have breakfast with him. This was the very day for the fort to be given up and the sudden return of Washington frightened Arnold. Just before his guests arrived, a messenger brought word of André's capture. Hastily bidding his wife good-by, he flung himself on his horse and galloped away. After breakfast, Washington went on with Rochambeau to the fort. No salute welcomed them. General Arnold was not there and apparently they were not expected. While wondering at his absence, Washington had no thought of treachery. Then Hamilton brought him the dreadful news. "Whom can we trust now?" was all he said. Hamilton rode hard after Arnold, but he escaped to the British ship which was lying in the river.

Major André endeared himself to everybody by his charming manners, intelligence and bravery. The young officers loved him and the British made every effort to save him, but honorably refused to give up General Arnold in exchange for him. Washington treated André with the greatest kindness, but justice to America required that this fine young officer should die and he suffered the shameful death of a spy (October 2, 1780). His body was later sent to England and he was buried in Westminster Abbey. General Arnold was made an officer in the British army, but nobody trusted him, and the men hated his command. Twenty years afterward (1801), he died, poor and broken-hearted, in a foreign land. It is said that, on his death-bed, he called for his old American uniform and asked to be allowed to die in it. "God forgive me," he cried, "for ever putting on another!"

Count Rochambeau had told a pretty story about his journey from Newport with General Washington. One evening, as they passed through a large town, the people came out to greet their General. Throngs of children carrying torches crowded about him, touching his hands and calling him "Father." He was very kind and gentle to all these people, but the patriotism of the children pleased him most. He said Great Britain could never conquer a country whose children were taught to be loyal.

Another French officer said of Washington's horses, "They are as good as they are beautiful, and all perfectly trained. He trains them all himself. He leaps the highest barriers and rides very fast." At one time, early in the war, when the Virginia riflemen first came north, some Marblehead (Mass.) fishermen laughed at their fringed hunting shirts and a fight followed. Washington heard of it, jumped on his horse and galloped into camp. His colored servant was going to let down some bars for him, but he leaped over them and dashed into the midst of the fight. He seized the two biggest riflemen and shook them, commanding peace.

Washington, as usual, was prevented, through lack of men and supplies, from giving the British a blow. Months passed without much being done, except dashing skirmishes now and then. The two camps watched each other, wondering what the other would do.

Washington bidding Farewell to His Officers

CHAPTER VII

GENERAL GATES DEFEATED AT CAMDEN, S. C.—BATTLE OF KING'S MOUNTAIN—WASHINGTON SENDS AID TO THE SOUTH—SIEGE OF YORKTOWN—SURRENDER OF LORD CORNWALLIS—PEACE TREATY SIGNED—WASHINGTON'S FAREWELL TO HIS OFFICERS—1780-1783

Though Washington did not have any encounters with the British for a long time, the Americans were engaged in bitter fighting in the South. Lord Cornwallis angered the people of South Carolina by hanging a number of prisoners at Charleston and by the cruel raids of General Tarleton and his dragoons, who rode about the country, slaying innocent people. General Thomas Sumter, who was nicknamed the "Game Cock," gathered together a few men. Those who had no guns sharpened their saws into swords and fastened hunting knives on long poles and thus armed, these soldiers gave the British a great deal of trouble.

Meanwhile, General Lincoln was still held a prisoner of war and the people were very glad when they heard that General Gates, the hero of Saratoga, had been sent to take command of the Southern forces of the American army. Gates was very headstrong, however, and thought he knew more than any one could tell him and would take no advice from officers on the ground. He did the worst thing he could do—he rushed at once into an open battle with Lord Cornwallis (August 16, 1780) and met with a terrible defeat at Camden, South Carolina.

Cornwallis now marched into North Carolina to subdue that State. Her Scotch-Irish people, always brave, had declared themselves independent of Great Britain a whole year before Congress had dared to do so. Cornwallis found himself in a "hornets' nest." Sharp-shooters and bold riders cut off his messengers and foraging parties. In the western part, the mountain people gathered, who were used to Indian fighting. They were joined by rugged men from all parts of the South. Each man was dressed in homespun, with a deer's tail or bit of green stuck in his hat. Each carried a long rifle, hunting knife, knapsack and blanket. At King's Mountain (on the border line between North and South Carolina), this little army overtook and destroyed a British and Tory force under General Ferguson. Soon after, Lord Cornwallis retreated to South Carolina again.

The victory at King's Mountain aroused all the patriotism of the mountain folk. Francis Marion, one of the bravest soldiers of the South, took the field with a brigade of friends and neighbors. Armed with knives and rude swords, he, like Sumter, would surprise and capture British posts and then gallop back to the woods, while the enemy would be at a loss to know where he came from. The British called him the "Swamp Fox."

About this time, Colonel William Washington, a kinsman of the General, with a few horsemen, surprised a body of Tories who had made their headquarters in a log barn. He put the trunk of a tree on two wagon wheels, painted it to look like a cannon, and pointed it at the barn. Then he sent a messenger with a white flag of truce to tell them to surrender or be blown to pieces. Their leader and one hundred and twelve men surrendered! They felt very foolish when they saw the cannon and were laughed at all over the State.

General Gates, broken-hearted over his defeat at Camden, was trying to gather up his scattered army. To add to his sorrow, he received word that his only son was dead, and soon after, he was notified that Congress had given his command to General Greene and ordered an investigation of his defeat. These troubles were almost more than he could bear, but his feelings were soothed by a letter from General Washington, full of tender sympathy and expressions of confidence. The letter so comforted him that he was found in his room kissing the words. General Greene was also very considerate, and the proud heart of Gates, who had wronged both these men, was melted, by their kindness, into lasting love for them.

General Greene found the army small and discouraged, but he soon inspired the men with renewed hope. He had with him the famous Virginia Rifles under General Daniel Morgan, who had served bravely at Quebec and Saratoga. This division was attacked at Cowpens (S. C.) January 17, 1781, by Tarleton and his large force, but Morgan was so daring and skillful that he routed the British, who lost 800 of their 1100 men.

Cornwallis tried to attack General Greene, who knew his army was too small to risk a battle; so he led Cornwallis a long chase through forests and mountains, while his light horse troops under Harry Lee annoyed the British like wasps that sting and fly away to return and sting again! Greene was at last overtaken and defeated, but the effect of the battle so crippled the British that there was nothing for them to do but retreat to the nearest sea-coast town, where they might get aid from their fleet. General Greene marched hard after them, turning his defeat into a victory, and so hampering Cornwallis that he lost hope.

Cornwallis now turned northward into Virginia and Greene gave up the chase and marched into South Carolina. He, with Lee, Marion, Sumter, Wade Hampton and other daring officers, fought battle after battle until they had regained from the British most of Georgia and the Carolinas (September, 1781).

In Virginia, Lafayette and "Mad Anthony" Wayne kept annoying Cornwallis as he marched to Portsmouth on the James River.

Meanwhile Washington, while giving advice and directing the campaigns in the South, where he had sent some of his most brilliant generals, was watching General Clinton. Ever since the Battle of Monmouth (N. J.), he had remained in the neighborhood of New York. Though he was needed with his army in the South, he dared not leave the Hudson unguarded. At last, however, he planned to help the South by causing the British to recall some of their troops. He had the French forces come and encamp near his army, and appear to be making arrangements for laying siege to New York. Even the soldiers thought they were going to try to take the city. General Clinton fell into the trap and wrote to Cornwallis for all the regiments he could spare. Troops were hurried aboard ship and set sail for New York.

Clinton found out, too late, how completely he had been deceived, for Washington and Rochambeau slipped out of their camps and marched their armies across New Jersey! He took his revenge by sending Benedict Arnold, who was now a British officer, to his native State, Connecticut, to plunder and lay waste the country and murder the garrisons. This brutality was Arnold's last act in America, and shortly after, he went to England.

When the French and Continental armies reached Philadelphia, they were received with rejoicing. Washington was entertained in the home of Robert Morris, a patriot banker, without whose help, in raising money, Washington could not have saved the country and who more than once had come to the aid of the army. At this time, he loaned the government $20,000 in gold, and at about the same time, France sent the colonists more than a million dollars in coin.

The Continental army paraded through Philadelphia (August 30, 1781), dusty and ragged, but keeping step to the fife and drum. The next day, the French troops marched through, jaunty in white and green uniforms, with bands playing. Lafayette, who was in Virginia, sent word to Washington that the British troops had landed at Yorktown (instead of going to New York), and that Cornwallis was strongly fortified there. The British battleships lay in the river before the town. Cornwallis thought his only enemy was Lafayette, of whom he had little fear. Lafayette carefully arranged his troops to cut off any retreat from

Yorktown, and waited for Washington. A powerful French fleet arrived from France and bottled up Cornwallis in the York River. The American and French armies marched on from Philadelphia, Washington taking time on the way to visit Mount Vernon, which he had not seen for six years.

**Washington spent the first
night under a mulberry tree**

Cornwallis felt very safe and snug in Yorktown (Va.) till he saw the French ships, and then he decided to retreat. But every way was blocked. The allied armies (American and French) entrenched themselves close about the town. Washington spent the first night among his men sleeping under a mulberry tree. On the night of October

6th (1781), the siege of Yorktown began, Washington himself putting the match to the first gun. A week later, two strong British redoubts (forts) were stormed and taken, one by an American company under Colonel Hamilton and the other by the French. The British kept up a constant bombardment of the American lines, and Washington was often in the greatest peril. On one occasion, an officer spoke of his danger and Washington said, "If you think so, you are at liberty to step back." He was never afraid and what the Indian had said of him years ago seemed indeed true.—"A mighty Power protected him and he could not die in battle!"

The Americans pounded the British fortifications to pieces. Cornwallis looked in vain for help from New York. He was surrounded on all sides and all hope of escape was gone. On the 19th of October, 1781, in order not to sacrifice the lives of any more of his brave men, Lord Cornwallis surrendered to General Washington. The whole country went wild with joy over this great victory, and the Americans did not forget that the French, with their men, money and ships, made it possible for them to win. The troops held services of thanksgiving in camp, and Congress named a day when all the people should thank God. When Cornwallis surrendered, Washington treated the British with great kindness and courtesy.

The English were now having so much trouble in Europe that it was difficult for them to carry on the war in America; but they were not willing to make peace on terms that America would accept. Washington thought that the only way to secure a glorious and lasting peace was to be prepared to carry on the war. If the British should see the colonists weak and unprepared, they would either conquer them or offer them an inglorious peace. He, therefore, fortified his forces at Newburgh on the Hudson, where they were joined by the French.

The entire year 1782 was spent in camp. The men soon became discontented. Congress and the States were slow, as usual, in furnishing supplies. But Washington's patience and fair dealing kept the men loyal to him and the country.

The first articles of peace were signed in France, November 30, 1782, but it was not until September 3, 1783, that the final treaty of peace with England was signed at Paris.

On April 19th (1783), just eight years after the Battle of Lexington, Washington proclaimed to his troops that the war was over; but the British did not leave New York until November, and then Washington and the Governor marched in.

Mrs. Betsy Ross

On December 4, at Fraunce's Tavern, New York City, he said good-by to the officers and men who had served and suffered so long with him; there were tears in his eyes and theirs, as he shook their hands and bade them farewell. A ship carried him to Annapolis, Maryland, where he surrendered his commission to Congress. He said, "I close this last act of my official life by commending the interests of our dearest country to the protection of Almighty God and those who have the superintendence of them to His holy keeping." He sheathed his sword after years of faithful and honorable service. Through good and evil fortunes, he had always held firmly to ideals of truth, courage and patriotism, and he retired from public life admired and loved by his countrymen. He arrived at Mount Vernon on Christmas eve (1783).

The United States now had a place among the nations of the world. She had a flag of her own, the beautiful Stars and Stripes, created in the dark days of the war. For a hundred and fifty years, the colonies had used the flag of Great Britain. When the Revolution broke out, each State and regiment had its own flag; but in 1777, Congress appointed Washington, Robert Morris and Colonel Ross a committee to devise a flag. They were in Philadelphia at the time, and it was in the house of Betsy Ross (which still stands) that the first American flag was made, consisting of thirteen red and white stripes, with a circle of thirteen white stars on a blue field, "representing a new constellation." (A group of fixed stars.) This flag was accepted by Congress on June 14, the day that is now celebrated in the United States as Flag Day.

Washington Welcomed in New York

CHAPTER VIII

WASHINGTON RETIRES TO MOUNT VERNON—INAUGURATED AS FIRST PRESIDENT OF THE UNITED STATES—HIS REËLECTION—HIS DEATH AT MOUNT VERNON—1783-1799

The Dome of the Capitol at Washington

There are many things to be remembered about the Revolution. Its objects were to gain liberty, equality and a fair chance for everybody. It was won by the patience and courage of patriots, ill-fed, ill-clad and ill-paid. Its armies were too weak for the glory of many great battles. Years afterward, Lafayette said to Napoleon, "It was the grandest of causes, won by the skirmishes of sentinels and outposts."

Washington laid aside his sword and spent five happy years at Mount Vernon. He was a brave soldier, but he loved best the quiet life of the farm. He once said, "How pitiful is the ambition which desolates the world with fire and sword for the purpose of conquest and fame, compared to making our neighbors and fellowmen happy!"

81

His home was filled with guests whom he loved to entertain and who were always sure of a courteous and dignified welcome. The two little children of Mrs. Washington's son (who had died of fever during the war), Nelly and George, made the place merry and the General joined in their play and enjoyed the change from camp to home life. Those who were with him constantly say that he never spoke of himself and never referred to any of his battles. He had done his work and done it well. Now he left it behind him and looked forward to the joy of his home. At the close of the war, some of his friends had wanted to make him king, but he would not hear of it. He had fought to make America a free land, and not for his own glory.

Washington spent five happy years at Mount Vernon

The thirteen States were loosely bound together in a Confederation. As time went on, the rights of different States came into conflict. Washington, from his fireside, watched the interests of his country. He believed with other great Americans that only a strong central government could keep harmony among the States. In 1787, a convention was called in Philadelphia to talk the matter over. Each State sent its most brilliant and thoughtful men, among them, of course, being Washington. After four months of careful consideration and labor, they offered to the American people the glorious Constitution, upon which has been built up the great Republic of the United States. Washington said they had God's help in "laying the foundation for tranquillity and happiness." The people accepted the Constitution and turned to Washington for their first President. No one else was thought of, and he was unanimously elected. New York was chosen for the capital.

Before he left Virginia, Washington went to say farewell to his mother, knowing he would never see her again. She was old and feeble, but happy to see her son so useful and so honored. She always said, "He is a good son and has done his duty as a man."

As Washington journeyed to New York, people thronged the roadsides. Bells rang and cannon roared. Soldiers and citizens escorted him from city to city. At the lower end of New York Bay, he was received on a splendid barge, which led a procession of boats gay with flags and music. At the pier, he was met by the Governor of the State.

On April 30, 1789, Washington took the oath of office on the open balcony of Federal Hall, in Wall Street, in the presence of a great multitude. Then he walked to St. Paul's church and devoutly kneeling, prayed to God for strength and guidance.

Washington had need to pray, for he was facing difficulties and problems greater than any he had known. He was at the head of a government, such as had never been tried before, and the eyes of the world were upon him. The peoples of down-trodden lands looked to him for the success of freedom. He said truly, "I walk untrodden ground," for there was no great republic in history whose example he could follow. His heavy task was to bring into harmony the differences of widely separate States; to make fair laws; to create a national money; to organize the different departments of government—in short, to make one nation out of thirteen.

Washington never flinched from responsibility. He took up his new work with methodical patience, and was most fortunate in having the help of great men. The States sent their best men to Congress. John Adams was Vice-President. The first Secretary of State was Thomas Jefferson, who had written the Declaration of Independence. General Knox was made Secretary of War. The still youthful Alexander Hamilton was appointed Secretary of the Treasury; the country owes much to him for its success and prosperity, for he was the one who made the financial plans, without which the government could not exist.

Federal Hall

Washington's family joined him in New York, where they lived. The city streets were dirty and dark at this time and only one was paved. Negro slaves carried all the water for the household from the river, in tubs balanced on their heads, while drinking water was sold from wagons, as there was only one pump in the city. The President traveled about in a cream-colored coach with pictures painted on the doors and panels. It was drawn by cream-colored horses with white manes and tails. Sometimes on Saturday afternoons, this coach, which was well known to all the people, was sent to bring playmates to drive with Nelly and George.

Washington drove to the first meeting of Congress in a coach drawn by six horses, with a coachman and footman in scarlet and white liveries, and with an escort mounted on prancing white steeds. Such style really was not uncommon in those days and the six horses were not so much for show as they were needed to draw the heavy carriage over the bad roads. The fear that our country might become a monarchy had not entirely disappeared, so Washington lived as simply as he could and avoided everything that suggested the pomp of a king.

The President and Mrs. Washington often went on foot to call on their friends, and that the people might meet them freely, they held public receptions on Friday evenings from eight to ten. While always reserved and dignified, Washington was gracious and attentive to his guests. His wife was the same sweet hostess as at Mount Vernon. At dinner, if no chaplain was present, Washington asked the blessing himself. Sunday was always strictly observed in the Washington household. In the morning, the President went to church, and the rest of the day he spent quietly with his family. In the autumn after his election, he wrote the first Proclamation setting aside a Thursday in November for Thanksgiving. From that time to this, in November of each year, America gives thanks to God for her liberties.

At this time, Lafayette was fighting for the cause of liberty in France. When the terrible Bastille prison in Paris was torn down at his command, he sent its huge key to Washington, because he believed the same love of liberty, for which Washington had fought, had also destroyed this state dungeon of tyranny, where many good people had suffered unjustly.

One of the problems Washington had to meet was the warlike attitude of the Indians, with whom there was some border fighting. He always treated them fairly and often entertained them. When they came, he impressed them by a great show of elegance and style. Once a great chief and twenty-eight warriors from Alabama came to make a treaty. The President gave them a splendid dinner at his house. Then he showed them a full length, oil portrait of himself. They looked at it, touched it and looked behind it. Finding it flat, they grunted in disgust and not one of them would allow his picture to be made! Dressed in his handsomest clothes, the President took them, in their full dress of feathers and paint, for a walk down Broadway, which he enjoyed as much as they.

Washington liked to slip away from his cares and go fishing. He was a good fisherman and it was said "all the fish came to his hook."

The Southern States were not pleased with the choice of New York as the capital, as they thought it too far away; so the seat of government was moved to Philadelphia. Washington wanted to move quietly. On a summer morning, he and his family were all up by candle light, expecting to steal away in their carriages, when, suddenly, a military band began to play under their windows! The people came running from all directions. "There, we are found out!" said the President. "Well, they must have their way." So his party walked to the pier between rows of loving people, and were rowed to the Jersey shore, while cannon boomed and the multitude shouted. Six horses were needed to drag their coach over the poor roads and the occupants of the coach were in danger of being upset.

The house of Robert Morris, in Philadelphia, was taken for Washington, who paid the rent himself. Pennsylvania built a President's Mansion, but it was so big and fine that Washington refused to live in it, and so it was used for the Pennsylvania University.

While his furniture was coming by sea from New York, Washington had time for a short visit to Mount Vernon, but he and his family were settled in his new home when Congress met the first Monday in December.

About this time, two political parties began to form in the United States. The Federalists, who were led by Hamilton, wanted to make a strong central government, which would develop the country and be respected abroad. The Democratic-Republicans, who were led by Jefferson, wanted the States to hold the chief power, because they were afraid a strong central government might be turned into a monarchy. Both parties had the good of the country at heart. Jefferson's party is the Democratic Party of the present day and the Federalists live still in the Republican Party.

Jefferson and Hamilton were bitterly opposed to each other's ideas and disputed with their usual fighting quality. Washington quietly heard each side and did his best to keep the two men at peace, for the country needed both.

In the spring and summer of 1791, Washington made a tour of the Southern States. It was a trip covering eighteen hundred and seventy-five miles. The same horses made the entire journey and kept up their spirits until they trotted back into their stalls at home! The President returned very happy about the condition of the country and delighted with its confidence in the new government.

The end of his term of four years drew near and Washington looked forward to the comfort of private life. He was growing quite deaf and had had several severe illnesses. He was tired of the load of care, and of the strife of opposing parties. But four years were not time enough to establish so great a government. Washington alone held the faith and confidence of the people, and they begged him to give them four years more. He wanted to retire, as he feared that, after another term, he would not be able to carry out his plans for Mount Vernon; but he finally consented.

Washington's second term was filled with great difficulties. Indians attacked the western frontiers, and Algerian [Algeria is in northern Africa] pirates seized American ships and imprisoned American citizens. France and England were at war and it was difficult to keep America out of the quarrel. These and other problems, besides disputes among public men, kept Washington's heart weary and sore. Through it all, he said, "There is but one straight course and that is to seek truth and pursue it steadily." His only wish was to "lead the country to respectability, wealth and happiness." He paid no attention to his own comfort or desire. Though often misunderstood and ridiculed by men who did not agree with him, he never failed to do what he thought was right. His wisdom and justice were so great that, in all these years, the wisest men have found little in the actions of Washington they would change. Jefferson said of him that no motive of interest or friendship or hatred could influence him; "he was in every sense of the word a wise, a good and a great man."

At the close of his second term, 1797, Washington insisted upon retiring, and he counted the days until he might lay aside the cares of office and seek his rest. He sent his Farewell Address to Congress, and it has been said that nothing finer has ever been written than his last great message to his countrymen.

On the 4th of March, 1797, John Adams was inaugurated as the second President of the United States. But the thought and love of the great assembly at the inaugural ceremony were turned toward Washington, the white-haired soldier who had led the country through war to prosperous peace. The people followed him to his door, where, with tears in his eyes, the "Father of his Country" waved farewell to them and to all beloved citizens of the nation.

In a few days, Washington was at home again upon his farm. He spent his time riding over his plantations, looking after his crops and horses and cattle. Often he took out his surveying instruments and spent a day laying out his land, or he planted trees and vines about his house and lawns. To the country folks, he was a beloved neighbor and friend. Visitors came frequently to his home, while Nelly and George and their young friends kept the place lively. Under the care of her Grandmother, Nelly had grown into a beautiful and well educated young lady. Her wit and sweetness of temper were a great joy to Washington, who loved her dearly. She had many suitors, but delighted Washington by choosing his favorite nephew, Lawrence Lewis, for her husband. They were married on Washington's birthday and the General wore his old Continental uniform of buff and blue, though he had a new and finely embroidered one that Nelly wanted him to put on.

The quiet life of Mount Vernon was broken before long. The new President got into such trouble with France that the country was threatened with war. Washington was asked to take his old position of Commander-in-Chief of the army and he accepted. He organized an army, but, fortunately, peace was made without bloodshed, and he was glad to go back to Mount Vernon.

One winter day, while riding, Washington was caught in a heavy storm of rain and snow. He was used to all kinds of weather and thought nothing of the exposure, even though he was hoarse and had a severe cold the next day. Before morning of the third day, he was very ill and when the doctors came, they bled him. It was the stupid practice of those days and in a few hours Washington was so weakened as to be past hope of recovery. He died on December 14, 1799, as bravely as he had lived. His wife praying beside him was as brave and calm as he. He had asked that his funeral might be a simple one, and so it was. None was there but friends and neighbors. The casket was carried out upon the veranda that all might see his face. Troops from Alexandria, (Va.)

with solemn music led the funeral procession. Four clergymen in white followed. The General's favorite horse, with saddle and bridle, was led by two negro grooms. The casket, borne by Free Masons and army officers, was followed by his family, and by friends and neighbors. While minute guns were fired from a warship in the river below, the procession wound along the lovely paths of Mount Vernon to the family tomb on the hillside. Here the body was laid to rest with religious and Masonic ceremonies.

When the news reached the people that Washington was dead, the whole country went into deepest mourning. In Europe, the sorrow was true and sincere. The British fleets put their flags at half-mast and Napoleon ordered crêpe put upon the banners of France. Though Washington was born and educated in America and belongs truly to Americans, he was such a friend to humanity, such a champion of liberty, that the whole world claims him as a model.

His will provided that, after the death of his wife, all his slaves should be free and he left money for those who could not earn a living. His able management had made Mount Vernon a great estate of nine thousand acres. Beside this, he held forty-four other tracts of land in nine different States, and he was one of the greatest land owners in America. Believing that the Republic would stand secure only upon a foundation of education, courage and conscience, he left money for a great American University. In this, he wanted the young people to be trained in the principles of true Americanism. He wanted the intelligence of the country to guide its politics. It is unfortunate that, to the present day, the university has not been founded, although there is now every likelihood that such a National University will be established in Washington and vast sums contributed to the fund Washington had left for this purpose.

The site of the city of Washington was selected for the Federal Capital in 1790, and ten years later, the seat of government was moved from Philadelphia to Washington. President Washington himself headed the body of commissioners who chose the site and arranged for the purchase of the land. The city was named in his honor. It is beautifully laid out with magnificent avenues, parks, fountains and stately buildings, and is one of the finest and most comfortable cities in the world.

In the house at Mount Vernon, there was a little attic room, hot in summer, bitter cold in winter. But its one window was the only one that looked upon the tomb on the hillside, and so Mrs. Washington, after the death of her husband, moved into this little room. Two and a half years later, she died there and her body was laid beside that of Washington.

Washington's Tomb at Mount Vernon

Years passed and the beautiful house began to fall into ruin. A new and simple tomb was erected to Washington, but it also was neglected. Nothing was done to restore Mount Vernon until the women of the country bought the place. They rebuilt the walls and porches, brought back the old furniture, planted vines about the tomb, and still keep it as Washington would have wished, as a shrine for all to visit, where respect can be paid to the memory of the "Father of his Country."

Other books from Classic Books Publishing:

Romeo and Juliet by William Shakespeare
ISBN: 978 – 3 – 941579 – 00 – 2

Comedy of Errors by William Shakespeare
ISBN: 978 – 3 – 941579 – 01 – 9

Hamlet Prince of Denmark by William Shakespeare
ISBN: 978 – 3 – 941579 – 02 – 6

Julius Caesar by William Shakespeare
ISBN: 978 – 3 – 941579 – 03 – 3

Macbeth by William Shakespeare
ISBN: 978 – 3 – 941579 – 04 – 0

A Midsummer Night's Dream by William Shakespeare
ISBN: 978 – 3 – 941579 – 05 – 7

Adventures of Huckleberry Finn by Mark Twain
ISBN: 978 – 3 – 941579 – 06 – 4

Pride and Prejudice by Jane Austen
ISBN: 978 – 3 – 941579 – 07 – 1

Dracula by Bram Stocker
ISBN: 978 – 3 – 941579 – 08 – 8

Little Dorrit by Charles Dickens
ISBN: 978 – 3 – 941579 – 09 – 5

Great Expectations by Charles Dickens
ISBN: 978 – 3 – 941579 – 10 – 1

More under: www.ClassicBooksPublishing.com